I first met Barbara Stennes, Lifetime Certified de Bono Master Trainer, in 1992. She was a promising apprentice from the start and has since taught my thinking methods to thousands of individuals, helping to improve thinking in organizations around the world. Barbara became one of my first Master Trainers and is now one of only 3 Lifetime Certified de Bono Master Trainers worldwide. I personally trained and certified Barbara in Six Thinking Hats®, Lateral Thinking, and Direct Attention Thinking Tools®; and I count on her as a key proponent of my work.

Barbara came to me with the idea for *Innovation: Case-by-Case* in the fall of 2003. By the summer of 2004 she had collected stories from many groups around the world detailing wonderful work. All the stories share a central theme: how to apply new ways of thinking to get new—and better—results. I hope that *Innovation: Case-by-Case* will be the first of a series of collections published to recognize, encourage and support people who are changing the way the world thinks. You can become a part of this project by contacting Barbara or the publisher with your case report.

Edward de Bono

Dr. Edward de Bono

INNOVATION:
-Case-by-Case-

Six Thinking Hats

Lateral Thinking

DATT

How the de Bono Thinking Systems Have Transformed Companies Across the Globe

-Barbara Stennes- CSP

Published by
de Bono Thinking Systems
Des Moines, IA 50322
877-334-2687
©2004 by Barbara Stennes
Printed in the U.S.A.
Project Manager and Editor: Jennifer Chiaramonte
Graphic Design: Mike Aspengren
ISBN # 0-9755400-0-9

To the innovative clients and talented
de Bono trainers who generously offered their
success stories. Without them, this book
would not exist.

Acknowledgments

To Edward de Bono, whose brilliant work has brought me untold joy and gratification for the last 12 years. In case after case, I have seen the worldwide impact of his creative thinking methods, which inspired me to write this book.

For more than a decade, I've had the pleasure of working with many clients and colleagues around the world who are intensely passionate about creativity and innovation. Their commitment to the field of innovation has been remarkable. These stories are dedicated to them.

Amy Hoey, Emily Sennert, and Tiffany Gruver were ever so important during this process. They ably handled the technical and administrative areas of our office so that I might have time for interviews.

Thanks especially to Jennifer Chiaramonte for coming into my life at just the right time. Her coordination and persistence in meeting our deadlines was a major contribution to this project.

To my family members—you have been a constant source of support and encouragement throughout my life.

And, finally, I am grateful to Kathy Myers, who first introduced me to Edward de Bono's methods over 17 years ago. Her natural ability to see the full potential of people and projects has truly been an inspiration in my life and work.

Special Thanks

A very special thanks goes to each person who provided information for this book.

Jon Albregts	Melchor Batista	Massimo Soriani Bellavista
Susan Blouch	Lynda Brest	Alan Burns
Russell Chalmers	Lynda Curtin	Pamela Dimich
Chuck Dymer	Dina Faidi	Linda Finkelstein
Robert Fisher	Steve Fisher	Jerah Gallinger
Razia Garda	Sunil Gupta	Jim Horn
Jan Hovrud	Diane Hyde	Sally Jagnandan
Frank Jenio	Natalie Jenkins	Kim Johnson
Debbie Kenseth	Mary Lou Leistikow	Wolfgang Lux
Denyse Lynch	Valerie McGee	Diane McQuaig
Don McQuaig	Andreas Novak	Simona Popovici
Mary Beth Russell	Robin Ryde	Jim Schreier
Stuart Scott	Jesse Shearin	Mike Sproul
Patti Thompson	Grant Todd	Nicola Tyler
Jay Wenberg	Dianne White	

Table of Contents

Introduction

Dr. Edward de Bono is the world's leading authority on the direct teaching of practical management thinking. As a former Rhodes scholar at Oxford, de Bono earned his M.D. and Ph.D. He held appointments at Oxford, Cambridge, London and Harvard universities. He has written more than 60 books, and his work has been translated into 35 languages. His exclusive tools and methods have brought astonishing results to organizations both large and small across the globe. His teaching has affected individuals from a broad range of cultures, educational backgrounds, occupations and age groups.

Dr. de Bono has produced thinking techniques that are simple, practical and powerful. His Six Thinking Hats, Lateral Thinking and DATT (Direct Attention Thinking Tools) training courses are used in organizations of all sizes to change thinking behavior, leading to increased productivity, stronger teams and profitable innovation.

Many organizations across the globe have attributed their success and productivity in part to the use of de Bono tools. This book will take a closer look at some of their stories.

The Tools

The next six pages will serve as a brief introduction to Dr. de Bono's thinking methods. For additional reading about Six Thinking Hats, Lateral Thinking or DATT, see Appendix A.

Six Thinking Hats®

The Six Thinking Hats is a critical thinking tool that enhances creativity, communication and productivity for teams and individuals. It is used primarily in meeting facilitation as a control mechanism that maximizes and organizes thoughts to improve problem solving and decision making.

The difference between a brilliant and mediocre team lies not so much in their collective mental equipment, as in how well they use it to work together. By using the Six Thinking Hats, team members learn how to separate thinking into six distinct categories. Each category is identified with its own colored metaphorical "thinking hat." Mentally wearing and switching hats can easily focus and redirect thoughts, conversations and meetings.

Six Thinking Hats helps actualize the full thinking potential of teams. When used as a meeting management tool, Six Thinking Hats provides the disciplined process for individuals to be focused and to the point. Most importantly, it requires each individual to look at all sides of the issue.

Six Thinking Hats can neutralize employee rank and put everyone on an equal playing field. It can also prevent more domineering or talkative personalities from controlling conversation, and thereby decisions. It will ensure the more reserved team members get to voice their thoughts as well.

Six Thinking Hats

- **White Hat:** calls for information known or needed

- **Red Hat:** signifies feelings, hunches and intuition

- **Black Hat:** assesses risk—what might go wrong or why something may not work

- **Yellow Hat:** looks at the benefits and why an idea might work

- **Green Hat:** focuses on creativity—the possibilities, alternatives and new ideas

- **Blue Hat:** manages the thinking process

Lateral Thinking™

Lateral Thinking is a way of thinking that seeks a solution to a problem through unorthodox methods or elements that would typically be ignored by logical thinking.

Dr. de Bono divides thinking into two methods. The first is "vertical thinking." This is the process of using logic and has been the traditional, historical way of thinking. Logic is useful for tracing along known pathways to arrive at predictable results, but it does not produce new ideas.

The second method is "lateral thinking." This type of thinking involves disrupting a logical thinking sequence to arrive at the solution from a completely different angle.

It is not only through luck or hard work that people can arrive at breakthrough ideas. Businesses and organizations can develop breakthrough ideas on command using Lateral Thinking methods. These methods give a deliberate, systematic process that results in innovative ideas. In other words, creative thinking is a skill that can be learned. Teaching people to use lateral thinking adds strength to their natural abilities, which leads to increased productivity and profit. Today, better quality and better service are essential, but they are not enough. Creativity and innovation are the only engines that will drive lasting, global success in the marketplace.

Lateral Thinking Techniques

- **Alternatives:** using concepts as a breeding ground for new ideas (This tool helps people push beyond the obvious alternatives to create new choices.)

- **Focus:** targeting thinking (This is the discipline of defining a focus and sticking to it.)

- **Challenge:** breaking free from the limits of current assumptions (With Challenge, a person must act as though the present way of doing things is not necessarily the best.)

- **Random Entry:** inserting unconnected input to open up new lines of thinking

- **Provocation and Movement:** generating illogical statements and using them as stepping-stones to usable new ideas

- **Harvesting:** capturing creative output (At the end of a creative-thinking session, many people take note of only the specific ideas that seem practical and have obvious value. This tool helps save beginning ideas that, with work, may later become valuable.)

- **Treatment of Ideas:** developing ideas and shaping them to fit an organization or situation

DATT®

Direct Attention Thinking Tools provide 10 simple strategies for sharpening perception and focusing thinking in a more comprehensive, effective and efficient way. DATT expands the user's viewpoint. The tools create a framework for defining a situation and improving the ability to consider consequences before taking action.

Our modern lives—both business and personal—are fast-paced and action-oriented. We often confuse action with accomplishment, and thereby jump into an action without giving it enough thought. We simply start moving and see what happens. If the results are good, we keep going; if they are bad, we stop to clean up the mess we've created. Although action is better than standing still, this way of trial and error is still inefficient because the mistake rate can be extremely high.

Individuals and groups may use DATT to focus attention and amplify perception when analyzing a situation, conducting an investigation or clarifying the mind before making decisions and reaching conclusions. DATT is also extremely valuable during a conflict when both sides insist they are right. It can also be a powerful tool to create consensus in a large group environment.

DATT Tools

- **C & S**—Consequence and Sequel
  Look ahead to see the consequences of an action, plan, decision or rule

- **P.M.I.**—Plus, Minus, Interesting
  Ensure that all sides of a matter have been considered before a decision or commitment is made

- **RAD**—Recognize, Analyze, Divide
  Break a larger concept into smaller, more manageable parts

- **CAF**—Consider All Factors
  Explore all factors related to an action, decision, plan, judgment or conclusion

- **A.G.O.**—Aims, Goals, Objectives
  Focus directly and deliberately on the intentions behind actions

- **A.P.C.**—Alternatives, Possibilities, Choices
  Deliberately try to find other ways

- **O.P.V.**—Other People's Views
  Step into others' shoes

- **K.V.I.**—Key Values Involved
  Ensure that thinking serves personal values

- **FIP**—First Important Priorities
  Select the most important ideas, factors, objectives, consequences, etc.

- **DOCA**—Design/Decisions, Outcome, Channels, Action
  Direct attention to the outcome of the thinking and action that follows

Summary:

Boeing used Six Thinking Hats to erase partisan lines between union and management and to thoroughly analyze a challenge and come to a solution.

Challenge:

- Make more light-duty jobs available to employees returning to work after disability leave

- Ensure union approves all company changes

Method:

- Use Six Thinking Hats to develop an early retirement incentive package

- Rely upon the synergy created by Six Thinking Hats to ask for a Memorandum of Understanding from the union

Result:

- 258 employees participate in the incentive program

- Union accepts the Memorandum of Understanding

The Story:

Boeing is the world's largest producer of commercial jetliners, and Boeing jets make 85% of the world's commercial flights. So when Boeing Toronto, Ltd. faced an employee challenge in the late 1990s, the company needed to resolve it as quickly and efficiently as possible.

The issue involved employees who were returning to work after disability leave. Due to physical restrictions, these men and women needed light-duty jobs that would not cause physical strain. For instance, some employees could lift only a certain amount of weight, and some could stand for only a limited amount of time.

The problem was that entitlement to the light-duty jobs was strictly governed by union guidelines. Under union agreements, seniority determined who held those jobs, and most returning employees did not have the seniority rights necessary to acquire the positions.

To compound the problem, workers at Boeing Toronto were being laid off. In the unionized environment, the younger workers took most of the cuts while the older employees were protected. As a result, light-duty jobs were in even greater demand due to the average age of remaining employees. Yet more light-duty jobs still needed to be made available to the employees returning from disability leave.

The Joint Modified Work Committee was called upon to resolve this predicament. The committee, consisting of both union and management representatives, came up with a list of 24 possible solutions. Although this was a great start, the committee wasn't sure how to proceed from there. Certain suggestions were being favored depending on whether the idea had come from management or union. In deciding which ideas to implement, partisan lines needed to be erased so a win-win solution could be reached.

In order to overcome the deadlock, President Steve Fisher encouraged the joint committee to implement the Six Thinking Hats. Steve asked Dianne White, the Manager of Education and Training, to facilitate a Six Thinking Hats session that would thoroughly analyze a few of the best ideas. But there weren't merely "a few" ideas to analyze; there were 24. Dianne decided that the committee should first prioritize the 24 ideas, so she held a vote. Each committee member identified four favorite ideas to explore further, and then the most popular ideas were thoroughly evaluated using all Six Thinking Hats.

The solution broke the tension between union and management because everyone had an equal voice in the final decision. This de-politicized the environment, and made it possible to evaluate ideas on their own merit.

One of the top proposals involved an early retirement incentive package. If the senior union members could be convinced to retire early, light-duty jobs would be naturally freed up without hassle or resentment. After analyzing this idea using the Six Thinking Hats, the committee decided to implement it. They called it the Voluntary Exit Program, and the response to it was astounding. More than 250 people took advantage of the program.

However, this solution did not completely solve the problem. Even though more light-duty jobs were now available, those jobs were still awarded on the basis of seniority. The committee made a bold move and asked the union for a Memorandum of Understanding. This would enable seniority rights to be waived so that light-duty jobs could be reserved for those who needed them most.

The Memorandum of Understanding was a big breakthrough for the committee because changes in seniority rules were usually obtained through formal bargaining. This was a significant move away from a conventional method to a more compassionate approach. It occurred, in part, as a result of the synergy created by Six Thinking Hats. Participants had finally managed to set aside their personal agendas so everyone could work collaboratively toward a positive outcome.

Summary:

The Potawatomi Bingo Casino used Six Thinking Hats to transform staff meetings and prevent major crises during a large-scale event.

Challenges:

- Eliminate personal bickering and arguments during regular staff meetings

- Add structure to the final preparation meeting prior to the large-scale event

Methods:

- Allow only White Hat thinking in weekly staff meetings

- Use Red and Black Hats in meeting prior to large-scale event in order to learn staff feelings and concerns

Results:

- Staff meetings are only needed every other week and are cut from two hours to 30 minutes

- Precautions are taken to avoid problems during the event

The Story:

The Potawatomi Bingo Casino in Milwaukee, Wisconsin held two-hour staff meetings every Tuesday morning. When Jim Schreier was hired as the casino's Consulting and Training Director, he was asked to attend these meetings as often as he could. He quickly became discouraged with the meeting's chaotic structure. Jim found a lot of personal bickering and anger, both between individuals and between the various departments. The meetings wasted valuable time and money. During one of these meetings, the casino owner stepped in to observe. Afterwards, he walked over to Jim and said simply, "Fix this."

Jim implemented a new training schedule including a two-day Six Thinking Hats workshop for all managers, and a one-day Six Thinking Hats training session for all supervisors. The response to the training was overwhelmingly positive, and the supervisors asked if they too, could receive the full two-day workshop.

More than 100 employees experienced the Six Thinking Hats training, and it led to a drastic change in the weekly staff meetings. Jim had recognized that the actual purpose of the staff meeting was purely informational, so he asked that only White Hat thinking be used. Any Red Hat thoughts could be discussed at a time other than weekly staff meetings.

Before long, staff meetings were necessary only twice a month, and they lasted only 30 minutes. Meetings would occasionally be cancelled altogether if there was no new information to be shared. The casino owner personally thanked Jim for the impact that the Six Thinking Hats had made. The casino saved an estimated $51,000 annually by reducing the time managers spent in lengthy staff meetings.

Jim was later asked to be in charge of one particularly important staff meeting. The casino was hosting a $500,000 Bingo event, the first ever of its kind. From 10 a.m. to midnight, the casino would be flooded with 2,300 people who had paid $350 each to have a chance at the big prize. There would be smaller Bingo tournaments throughout the day, a formal dinner and a laser light show preceding the grand finale Bingo game. Participants were flying in on charter jets from across the U.S., and professional gamblers from Las Vegas were coming to be part of the action.

In preparation for the big event, a final staff meeting had been called. Jim wanted to use more than a simple White Hat structure for this particular meeting, and he proposed that they begin by using Red Hat instead. The General Manager didn't think this was necessary because he assumed that everyone was excited about such a large-scale production. Jim suggested that beginning with Red Hat might reveal other feelings that should be addressed.

All meeting participants were asked to give one or two words to describe their feelings. As Jim had guessed, the word "scared" became a theme. Jim then asked everyone to share a specific Black Hat challenge that might arise. Managers were worried about unforeseeable problems with the size of the crowd, the staff, the money, the food, etc. The food service manager worried that because the magnitude of the event demanded a long workday, there could be a large number of no-call, no-show employees. To remedy this potential problem, the General Manager asked for every department to overstaff by 10-15%.

The maintenance manager worried the casino might not have enough electrical power for the laser light show. If the power went out, everyone would have to evacuate because the casino would essentially lock down. After some investigation, the maintenance manager's fears proved to be valid. The casino would not be able to power the laser show, so they brought in a generator for the event. Thanks to the discussion of Black Hat concerns, disaster was avoided.

After Jim finished hearing Black Hat challenges, he moved on to a quick rundown for Green Hat response to the question, "What can you do to support your employees the day of the event so that customer satisfaction will be at an all-time high?" One manager said she would be at the door to greet her employees with free t-shirts. Another manager suggested handing out $10 bills to each employee as he or she arrived at work.

Jim chose to forgo the Yellow Hat, because the benefits of running a highly profitable event were obvious, so he ended the session with Blue Hat to draw conclusions, next steps and action items. The result? The day went smoothly, and the first ever $500,000 Bingo game was a success.

Summary:

Pittsburgh Plate Glass Company (PPG) used Six Thinking Hats to overcome competing interests and opinions in choosing an alternative business strategy and deciding whether to shut down a plant.

Challenges:

- Choose the best of four business strategies in only four hours

- Decide what to do about overcapacity and whether to shut down a plant

Methods:

- Use a specific timed Six Thinking Hats sequence for the four-hour meeting

- Hold a customized Six Thinking Hats training prior to an important two-day meeting

Results:

- Alternative business strategy is chosen in the allotted time

- Plant managers are able to participate freely in discussion and complete the meeting agenda ahead of schedule

The Story:

PPG is a leading global supplier of glass, fiberglass, coatings and chemicals. In October 2000, the company ran into a dilemma. A core business had become a commodity, and the market was saturated. The company needed a new business strategy.

The Vice President of this business unit, along with a business consultant, had developed four potential strategies, one of which would be presented to the executive board. The Vice President called a meeting to evaluate the strategies. Because the consultant had been through a one-day Six Thinking Hats course, he recommended that Jesse Shearin, a PPG employee and Certified de Bono Instructor, conduct the meeting.

Jesse's challenge was to guide 11 people through the four business strategies and reach a consensus in only four hours.

The group was diverse in rank and title, with specialties ranging from manufacturing to research to corporate marketing. This created competing interests and opinions, because the four strategies had different implications for different parts of the business. For example, some strategies included investing in research and development technology and exiting significant portions of the business.

Jesse began the meeting with a brief overview of the Six Thinking Hats. He explained that the group would use the Six Thinking Hats to evaluate one strategy per hour. Each hour would begin with a 20-minute White Hat presentation of the strategy. This would be followed by a 6-minute Yellow Hat session about how the strategy fits in with current business and a 6-minute Black Hat session on reasons the executive board might veto the idea. Then came an 8-minute Green Hat session on overcoming Black Hat concerns and strengthening Yellow Hat benefits. In conclusion, a 15-minute Blue Hat session would summarize the findings regarding the strategy at hand.

Amazingly, the meeting was adjourned before the four hours' time scheduled. The Vice President had a final decision to take to the company executives, and the meeting participants had extra time to spare before catching their flights.

Three months later, Jesse was again called in to facilitate. This time another PPG business unit had a problem with overcapacity. There were too many plants producing too little product, and the CEO had directed that something be done about it.

Shutting down a plant was an option to consider, although it was an unpopular choice. Closing a plant would affect manufacturing for the next three years. Then, if business picked up—as it was expected to—the company would be unable to meet the increased demand.

A two-day meeting with six plant managers was planned to discuss whether or not to close a plant. Because each of the plant managers was fearful that his or her plant could be the one shut down, they would be reluctant to participate in the discussion. To prevent this from happening, Jesse began the meeting with a customized three-hour Six Thinking Hats training session.

Using the Six Thinking Hats, each plant manager was able to speak freely, even when the topic was the benefit of shutting down his or her own plant. By the end of the first afternoon, the group had already accomplished the original agenda of the entire two-day meeting.

Since they were now ahead of schedule, the team was able to use the second day to discuss alternatives to plant shutdown. They used Green Hat to answer the question, "How can we reduce capacity now while retaining the ability to ramp back up quickly when demand increases?" One suggestion was to close down specific lines or sections of plants, rather than an entire plant. This way, the company would be ready in case they needed added capacity in the future. After generating other ideas throughout the morning on how to effectively close down specific lines, the meeting was adjourned. The meeting had ended three hours early, and no plants would be shut down due to their decision to adopt the partial-shutdown idea.

Using Six Thinking Hats, PPG was able to create synergy between meeting participants where there might otherwise have been insurmountable rigidity. In addition, they were able to effectively evaluate strategies, make an important decision, save time and support all interests and individuals in the company.

Summary:

An ice cream company used Random Entry to solve a problem with their direct store delivery.

Challenge:

- Keep ice cream the same temperature from the time it is made until it is put on the shelves of small convenience stores

Method:

- Use Random Entry during a meeting to find a totally new approach to the delivery problem

Result:

- The direct store delivery system is customized to the geographical needs of New York City

The Story:

A prominent company specializing in premium ice cream was having a problem with its delivery. Because of the ice cream's high fat content, keeping it at precisely the right temperature was critical; otherwise, the cream and oil would separate, ruining the ice cream.

The ice cream changed hands several times from the factory to the grocers' freezers, and the company needed to monitor and control the temperature carefully at every stage. Across most of the nation, this was not a problem. In New York City, however, the traffic congestion prevented delivery trucks from pulling up to the smaller convenience stores and unloading quickly and efficiently. All too often, the ice cream thawed and spoiled.

To deal with this challenge, the owners of the ice cream company called in the owners of the trucking company to discuss better ways to handle direct delivery in New York City. The ice cream company asked Certified de Bono Instructor Susan Blouch from the Computer Sciences Corporation to facilitate the meeting.

Susan wanted the group to come up with an entirely new concept—one that would completely eliminate the delivery dilemma. She separated the group into pairs and gave them the Random Entry: hobby. She told the pairs to ask themselves, "What is it about my own hobby that might help to solve this distribution problem?"

After a few minutes of discussion, one pair was especially excited to share an idea. A participant said, "My favorite hobby is boating, so we started thinking about boats. If a boat is too big to reach the shore, the person will get off the big boat and get into a smaller boat and row to shore." The group was unsure where the pair was headed with their simple, yet strange observation. "So we wondered... why couldn't we send bigger delivery trucks to the outskirts of a busy place like New York City, and then have smaller vehicles of some kind come off those bigger trucks so they could easily maneuver and transport ice cream into the heavily congested areas?" Everyone in the group laughed. But their laughter was followed with looks that said, "Why not?"

The group then explored the boat idea more fully in a Green Hat session. Some people suggested that golf carts or bikes with freezers attached to them could be the "little boats" in the scenario. The larger semitrailers could be stocked with golf carts or bikes, just like the boat analogy.

By the end of the day, the group had discussed a number of potential solutions and intriguing ideas but had not reached a definite conclusion. Several months later, however, Susan learned that they had implemented and perfected a plan deriving from the boat suggestion.

"Ours is the age which
is proud of machines that
think and suspicious of men
who try to."

— Howard Mumford Jones

Summary:

The Globe and Mail used Lateral Thinking to help design a new classified section, which led to an increase in ad sales.

Challenge:

- Stop ad sales from continuing their downward trend

Method:

- Use Lateral Thinking and Green Hat thinking to produce a new classified ad section

Result:

- Ad sales increase just three weeks after the section launch

The Story:

The Globe and Mail, which has a circulation of nearly one million people, is called "Canada's National Newspaper."

Newsprint costs doubled in 1999, resulting in a significant decrease in advertising sales and adding financial strain for *The Globe*. Managers wanted to reverse this trend by thoroughly examining their approach to classified ad sales. They were open to changing everything from the price of an ad to the design of the newspaper itself.

However, this examination process wasn't going to be easy. There were 80 staff members from advertising sales, production and support services involved, and all of them were offering up ideas. Such a broad range of interests seemed like a setback. However, Bob Harris, Advertising Sales Manager for Telemarketing, recognized the potential for such a diverse mix of people to become an asset if they were given the opportunity to learn about Lateral Thinking.

Bob asked MICA, a Toronto-based consulting company, to hold three creativity-training sessions for the team members. After using Lateral Thinking, the team reached a consensus on *The Globe's* next move. The team would develop a completely separate and new classified ad section called "Marketplace." This section would take the classified ads that had formerly been scattered throughout the newspaper and assemble them in a single location. After agreeing to create a unique section, the group needed to generate fresh ideas about the overall appearance of "Marketplace."

The team embarked on a Green Hat session so that even the newspaper's most traditional thinkers could have an opportunity to think outside the box. This session resulted in the contribution of an astounding 80 practical ideas for the new "Marketplace" section. The ads would be mixed with editorial content to attract readers. Instead of listing the ads numerically, they would be grouped thematically. New typeface and category icons would be designed to give the section a reader-friendly feel. The lines between ads would be removed, creating an easy flow.

After the introduction of "Marketplace," ad sales representatives were eager to market the benefits of the impressive new section to advertisers. Once the attractive design was shown to potential advertisers, sales representatives received a much warmer reception. Advertisers recognized their ads were more likely to be seen in the innovative, new "Marketplace." The sales staff saw a substantial increase in ad sales just three weeks after the section launch. Meanwhile, competitors saw a decrease in their ad sales.

The Globe and Mail's use of Lateral Thinking and Green Hat thinking was not only effective, but also time efficient. In the past, it had taken *The Globe* at least one full year to design or redesign a specific section of the paper. With the de Bono tools to guide the process, the section was unveiled after a mere four months.

"A man is not idle because
he is absorbed in thought.
There is a visible labor and
there is an invisible labor."

— Victor Hugo

Summary:

A first grade girl used Six Thinking Hats in a counseling session to help her express emotions, which led to improved school performance and overall behavior.

Challenge:

• Help an emotionally disturbed girl open up in counseling

Method:

• Use Red Hat thinking to encourage the girl to share her feelings

Result:

• Performance in school and behavior at home improves

The Story:

Certified de Bono Instructor Diane Hyde is a first grade teacher. One year, she had a student named Ann* in her class. Ann's mother had completely abandoned her family several years earlier, leaving Ann's home life very chaotic. Ann's father had quickly remarried, and Ann and her younger siblings were still adjusting to their new stepmother.

Since beginning first grade, Ann had been having trouble completing her assignments and focusing in class. In addition to her academic problems, Ann had mounting behavioral problems. At times, she would hit classmates for no apparent reason, and she was giving her stepmother a lot of trouble at home.

In an attempt to become more involved in Ann's life, her stepmother started volunteering in the classroom for two hours each week. Ann's stepmother became acquainted with the Six Thinking Hats because Diane had incorporated them into her teaching process in Ann's classroom. The first graders enjoyed the concept of pretending to wear a different colored hat for each type of thinking they were told to use.

Ann's behavior and study habits grew worse each day. Ann's stepmother began taking her to counseling, but Ann would not share anything with the counselor. She was virtually mute during her sessions, even with her stepmother along to help her feel more relaxed.

*Name changed

One session, Ann was again refusing to tell the counselor any of her thoughts or feelings. Her stepmother suggested, "Ann, will you please put on your Red Hat and tell us everything you feel about me, your father and your mother?" At this point, Ann sat up, put on an imaginary hat and instantly started crying. She began talking about all her fears, guilt and confusion. She spoke for quite some time. It was the most Ann had ever shared with either her stepmother or her counselor.

The counselor couldn't believe how much one offhanded suggestion had altered the complexion of the counseling session. After hours without any type of breakthrough, an imaginary hat had ushered one in. The counselor asked Ann's stepmother to explain the Hat methodology. The counselor was extremely impressed that the Six Thinking Hats were being taught in a first grade classroom, especially after seeing what a tremendous impact they had on a child.

After the incident in the counseling session, everyone began to see a dramatic improvement in Ann's grades and behavior. It was as though the permission to release her feelings using Red Hat has allowed Ann to eliminate pent-up rage so she could begin looking for positive, rather than negative, reinforcement from the adults in her life. Ann's stepmother also noticed a drastic change in her behavior at home. Ann was happier and talked about her emotions more freely. Six Thinking Hats, although useful in business environments, can also be helpful in personal decisions and crises, regardless of a person's age.

"It is not enough to have a good mind. The main thing is to use it well."

— Descartes

Summary:

J. Walter Thompson used Six Thinking Hats to devise a unique promotional campaign that appealed to a specific age group.

Challenge:

- Create a campaign for the Ford Focus that would get noticed by 18- to 25-year-olds

Method:

- Use Six Thinking Hats to encourage new ways of thinking

Result:

- 100% more ideas than usual were generated by the team, leading to a winning idea that connected with the target group

The Story:

J. Walter Thompson is an advertising agency, founded in 1864, that boasts such accounts as Kraft, Kellogg's, Nestlé and Ford. The advertising team on the Ford account was given the task of creating a fresh ad campaign that would position the Ford Focus as a highly desirable car to the 18- to 25-year-old demographic. This target market is very difficult to reach because traditional television and print ads have little effect. People in this age bracket respond better to 'word of mouth' advertising.

The advertising team began its strategic planning meetings and could not come up with any totally new ideas. The account manager asked MICA, a Toronto-based consulting company, to teach the Six Thinking Hats to the team. Before learning the Six Thinking Hats, the team had too many strong and diverse opinions to reach a consensus. Using the new tools, collaboration in creativity moved the process beyond its initial stages.

Instead of days of endless meetings, a single, three-hour meeting solidified the details of the new campaign.

The team decided to build a campaign around music. Ford would sponsor the three-day Detroit Electronic Music Festival, as well as the Area 1 Alternative Music Tour. Black Hat thinking revealed that the typical banners and stickers at events such as these would not elicit the results the team hoped to achieve with this target market. Under Green Hat, they decided to put up a large tent that would double as a dance club. Two Focus cars would be parked outside the tent. These cars, each containing $20,000 worth of stereo equipment, would essentially be "rolling speakers." A DJ would then mix music, using the cars as speakers. There would also be "Fashion in Focus" dancers who would wear outfits constructed from pieces of the car. In addition, a computer kiosk would feature interactive games where a person could "drive" his or her own Ford Focus.

The tents proved wildly successful. At any given time, there were at least 100 people lined up, waiting to get inside the tents to hear about the Ford Focus. The advertising team gave Six Thinking Hats much of the credit, even referring to the method as its "creative caffeine." They continued to use the tools to design other successful ad campaigns.

"All too often we are stuffing the heads of the young with the products of earlier innovations rather than teaching them to be innovative.
We treat their minds as storehouses to be filled rather than as instruments to be used."

— Robert Finch

Summary:

The UK government used Six Thinking Hats and Direct Attention Thinking Tools in a training course to help unemployed youth.

Challenge:

• Teach unemployed young people better techniques for finding a job

Method:

• Provide a course as part of the government's Gateway to Work program using Six Thinking Hats and Direct Attention Thinking Tools

Result:

• Students report personal success in finding jobs

The Story:

In the 1990's, there were more than three million unemployed people in the UK. To cope with this problem, in 1998, the British government launched a program called Gateway to Work. The goal was to provide education and training for 18- to 24-year-olds who were without jobs.

As part of Gateway to Work, de Bono Master Trainer Stuart Scott was asked to lead a two-week training course. This course consisted of three sessions, two hours each, based on the Six Thinking Hats and Direct Attention Thinking Tools. The course was named "Thinking Smarter, Not Harder."

Stuart led the students through the Six Thinking Hats with an emphasis on creativity. He also included five of the Direct Attention Thinking Tools, which were linked back to the Hats. For instance, the CAF tool was linked with the White Hat for more information, while the O.P.V. and the C & S tools were linked to the Yellow and Black Hats.

During Green Hat discussion, students typically came up with about 40 nontraditional and creative ways of locating work, in comparison to the 8 ideas that would arise using normal thinking.

Many of the students were illiterate and had low self-esteem. Stuart believed the key to keeping the students' attention was to weave numerous true illustrations into the material, laced with a lot of wit and humor.

By listening to Stuart explain how the tools had helped him and others in both personal life and business, the class began to realize there might be hope in learning to think differently. New thinking skills were something they could all learn and use regardless of background or level of education. With new thinking skills, they could actually gain an edge on the competition for the jobs they desired.

During the course, each student explained his or her greatest challenge in finding work. The class then gave input, using the tools to overcome the problem. When the course was completed, every student received a small, plastic pocket card with the Six Thinking Hats and DATT explained on it. This card served as a visual reminder and useful reference.

The course produced numerous success stories. Paul had dropped out of school at age 16 and had no sustained periods of employment thereafter. His ideal job would be working in a recording studio, but he had met rejection after rejection.

The class proposed that instead of simply looking for openings in magazines and newspapers, Paul should visit recording studios in the area and tell them he was willing to perform any type of work. Paul followed this advice and was actually offered a job. The only problem was that Paul would not be compensated monetarily for his work. He would receive food and travel money, as well as free college tuition, but no additional pay.

Soon after Paul received this job offer, he was presented with another opportunity: a high-paying job at a factory. Paul was ecstatic that he now had two job opportunities but was unsure which one to take. He was leaning toward the factory job but decided to use the Six Thinking Hats to help make his final decision.

As a result, he decided to take the studio job and find another way to generate supplemental income. Using the Green Hat, Paul then developed a list of ideas to earn money in his spare time. He began a small but profitable weekend business of buying and selling car parts. This solution provided him financial stability while enabling him to pursue his ideal career.

Peter was another man who attended the course. He was a skilled carpenter who had been out of work for a long time. During class, Peter explained that he wanted to apply for a specific job he saw in the paper, but the company was too far from his house, and he did not drive. The class suggested Peter apply anyway, and if he got the job he could carpool with a fellow employee. Peter applied and was offered the job, but learned that no one in the company lived near him.

Rather than giving up, Peter used his new thinking skills to devise an alternative solution. He called the company next door and explained his situation to their personnel department. They were able to offer him names of several employees who lived near him, and Peter found a man willing to carpool.

Only six hours of training with the tools caused a complete shift in the students' thinking, leading them to job success. "Thinking Smarter, Not Harder" has been so successful that it is now offered to anyone, regardless of age, who has been out of work for six months or more. And due to Gateway to Work and other efforts, the unemployment numbers in the UK have dropped from three million to below one million, the lowest level in more than 25 years.

Summary:

GPIC used Direct Attention Thinking Tools to bring up
new questions and help them anticipate industry changes.

Challenge:

• Develop a list of potential problems to be addressed
  and analyzed

Method:

• Use DATT to help analyze challenges

Result:

• All factors are considered to avert future problems

The Story:

Gulf Petrochemical Industries Co. has been a successful producer of ammonia and methanol since 1987. In 1996, GPIC was named the best operation in the Arabian Gulf (a.k.a. Persian Gulf) in recognition of its record in production, employee safety and environmental standards.

The GPIC management team wanted to gain an additional edge in the industry so it brought in Master Trainer Sunil Gupta to teach a course in DATT. Management began using the tools immediately to anticipate change and improve the company's performance.

Using the CAF tool, the management team discussed the fact that the price of natural gas was soon going to double. Further analysis led them to the conclusion that the cost of electricity, steam and water would also increase. They decided to take additional measures to conserve water and electricity inside the plant.

Management used the P.M.I. tool to evaluate the suggestion that day-shift employees be given more flexible hours. The Plus points included less traffic on GPIC roads and happier employees. The Minus points included possible interdepartmental confusion; meetings could be affected, and information might be harder to relay, resulting in a communication breakdown. One Interesting point would be to watch how the employees might handle a new change in culture. Would they make a commitment to internal communication despite the inconvenience?

Using the O.P.V. tool, the managers asked themselves if GPIC should alter any day-to-day functions due to the war in a neighboring country. They asked each department to make suggestions. The managers suggested security be tightened and that everyone be more vigilant around the GPIC complex. Plant Operations asked that the ammonia inventory be reduced. The Technical Services crew suggested they devise a means to get rid of this excess ammonia. Safety and Security proposed taking greater precautions with any new visitor to the complex. Finally, Maintenance said they would arrange for any materials necessary to carry out these new modifications in the daily work process.

Because of DATT, GPIC was able to anticipate changes and begin to consider all factors and suggest solutions before problems arose. The tools have since become an invaluable part of their culture and are used by all managers in many situations.

"The major challenge
for leaders in the
twenty-first century
will be how to release
the brain power of their
organizations"

— Warren Bennis

Summary:

The University of New Brunswick used the Six Thinking Hats to solve a labor-relations problem, and Zayed University used the Six Thinking Hats to gain support for an employment program.

Challenges:

- Overcome the mutual distrust of administrator and union representatives during negotiations
- Hire more local workers without alienating current employees

Results:

- Negotiations go smoothly
- Incentives offered to employees willing to give up jobs

The Story:

Jim Horn was the Human Resources Director for the University of New Brunswick, which is one of Canada's oldest universities. As the University's chief negotiator, Jim had reached a four-year collective bargaining agreement for the school. This was somewhat risky, because the budget was established annually. However, the long-term contract would provide some stability for planning.

Jim had already trained the top university administrators in the Six Thinking Hats, and he wanted to train the faculty as well. One year into the four-year agreement, Jim delivered a Six Thinking Hats overview at a meeting of union executives. No further training took place.

Two years later, the University ran into a major problem. Due to cuts in government funding, the University was over-budget. Faculty tenure provisions prohibited restricting faculty salaries.

The University negotiators arranged a meeting with the union representatives. Although it had been two years since the faculty received the Six Thinking Hats overview, the union president opened the meeting by saying, "I'm putting on my Green Hat." Jim was amazed that two years after a brief introduction to Six Thinking Hats, the tools were still fresh in the mind of the union president. Everyone understood that the union president was signaling his willingness to discuss completely new ideas. This sidestepped the usual, confrontational model of negotiation, allowing numerous options to be considered without any commitment. Using the Six Thinking Hats process, it took only 15 minutes for the group to resolve the issue, and the union voted to approve the agreement.

A few years later, Jim became the Human Resources Director for Zayed University. Zayed University was established in 1998 in the United Arab Emirates. University employees came from across the globe, but the University had also implemented the National Development Program, which encouraged the hiring of U.A.E. citizens.

Jim was asked to improve the effectiveness of this program. Naturally, Jim could not simply ask current workers to train Emirates to take over their positions. The departments did not want to lose their knowledgeable and committed employees, so they resisted any change in staffing. The staff was paid well and received good benefits, so they had little interest in leaving their positions.

Jim had been trained in Six Thinking Hats, and he wanted to introduce the school's administration to the de Bono tools. He gathered together the university leadership, consisting of 75 of the most senior administrators. By exposing such a large number of people to Six Thinking Hats, Jim hoped to breed energy and commitment to help him meet the challenge.

Jim broke the administrators into small groups, gave them a structured Six Thinking Hats sequence to follow and asked them a set of questions. Afterwards, the large group reconvened to share output. Many of the issues that administrators would not normally voice came out during this thinking process.

The combination of using the Red Hat and a small group/large group process enabled the participants to speak more freely. A retirement incentive idea was eventually chosen as the perfect plan to jumpstart the National Development Program.

"People demand freedom of speech as a compensation for the freedom of thought which they seldom use."

— Soren Kierkegaard

Summary:

The Deliberation Skills Model™ used the Six Thinking Hats to improve juror decision making and reduce deliberation time.

Challenge:

- Create an alternative to the traditional process of discussion and conclusion in the jury deliberation room

Method:

- Introduce the Six Thinking Hats to jurors and judges before a trial, so the new framework can be used in deliberation

Result:

- Test trials prove successful in reducing conflict during deliberation

The Story:

After Certified de Bono Instructor Grant Todd served as a juror in a civil court case, he couldn't stop thinking about what had occurred in the deliberation room. Personality conflicts had created instant opponents. There was no organization to the discussion, and the jurors seemed to be primarily concerned with finishing as quickly as possible. Communication broke down as people began to take adversarial tones with one another. As the confrontation escalated, all reason seemed to dissipate.

Grant was also chosen to be the jury foreman and had grown frustrated as he noticed his behavior becoming more autocratic and heavy-handed. The experience left Grant wondering if there was a better way to handle jury deliberations, since the traditional process of discussion and conclusion did not seem to work well.

Grant had once heard about a Kentucky case in which the jury sentenced the defendant to death. After the trial, the judge asked the jury how everything had gone in the deliberation room. One bold juror answered, "All I know is that we'd still be arguing, had we not flipped a coin." It was a travesty of the legal system, but after what Grant had witnessed, he understood how jury deliberations could reach such extremes. Jury deliberation seemed to him to be a large blind spot in a revered American institution. Citizens were so poorly prepared for this civil duty that it was no surprise they were going to such lengths to get it over with.

Court cases are guided by a system of rules designed to bring all White, Black and Yellow Hat information to light. For this reason, it seems counterproductive for a jury to make a decision based exclusively on Red Hat thinking. The jury needs a systematic, comprehensive and balanced way to process information in what can be an emotionally charged setting.

Grant realized the core issue was being unable to manage conflict during deliberations. Without an agreed-upon discussion method for jurors, factions began to develop when there was a disagreement. This created an "us versus them" atmosphere, heightening the tension and leading to communication breakdown. The confrontation distracted jurors from the actual facts of the case and distorted their perceptions. From there, the situation spiraled further downward.

After Grant's experience as a juror, he began thinking about ways to apply the de Bono tools to judicial decision making. This led to Grant developing the Deliberation Skills Model in 2000.

Grant took all courtroom factors into consideration when developing the curriculum for the Deliberation Skills Model. Court officials would be offered a simple, brief overview of the process. These officials would then show the jury a quick half hour video to help them decide whether or not they wanted to use the model during deliberation.

With a new Six Thinking Hats framework in place, the group set a desired Hats sequence in which jurors can express their thoughts. This leads to greater participation from all jurors and makes it less likely that strong personalities will dominate discussion.

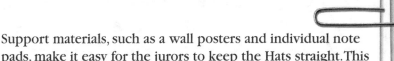

Support materials, such as a wall posters and individual note pads, make it easy for the jurors to keep the Hats straight. This process minimizes conflict and confusion, leading to clearer, more rational results in less time.

The role of the jury foreman is better defined. There are no delegation of roles, other than keeping time and recording comments. This allows each juror to participate fairly in the process. Because of this, the jury foreman finds it much easier to develop trust from fellow jurors.

After judges began hearing about the benefits of the Deliberation Skills Model, they expressed a desire for the same training to help them evaluate material during bench trials (a trial without a jury). As a result, the model was made available to both judges and juries.

The Deliberation Skills Model has been tested fifteen times in Michigan and Wisconsin, in both bench and jury trials. Jurors are interviewed after the trial, giving them the chance to explain benefits, problems or other aspects for process improvement.

The Deliberation Skills Model has been successful in reducing conflict during jury deliberations. Reports indicate improved juror focus, better communication and a reduction in deliberation time. This is only the beginning to what could be a national transformation in the jury deliberation process, leading to significantly positive and often life-changing outcomes.

Summary:

The Department of Natural Resources in Iowa used Six Thinking Hats to reduce customer calls by developing a vendor quick-reference guide. The tool was also used to resolve conflict within the DNR's Diversity Task Force.

Challenges:

- Reduce unnecessary phone calls to the DNR

- Decide whether to change the name of an existing task force

Methods:

- Use Green Hat to create a quick-reference guide for vendors so they can more effectively assist customers

- Develop a Six Thinking Hats worksheet for task force members to read prior to a meeting

Results:

- A decline in call volume

- Task force members arrive at a meeting ready to vote on name change

The Story:

The Department of Natural Resources in Iowa is in charge of the state's parks, forests, fish, wildlife, energy and water resources and environmental protection. The DNR receives 77,000 phone calls annually from the general public. In early 2003, the telephone operators realized that many of the calls came from people whose needs were not being met by the DNR's vendors, such as bait shops or sporting goods retailers. These customers should have gotten their answers directly from the vendors, but for some reason, they were calling the DNR instead.

A typical example might be a hunter who needs to renew his hunting education certificate. This simple procedure can be handled at any sporting goods stores. However, when the hunter goes to the store, the sales clerk is stumped by the relatively unusual request. He doesn't realize that a special computer code will generate the certificate renewal, so the clerk tells the hunter to call the DNR directly.

Acknowledging this predicament, the DNR Licensing Division sent letters to more than 3,000 vendors, instructing them to start meeting a greater variety of customer needs. Later, someone suggested that the letter might not have been an effective solution. The DNR Licensing felt partially responsible if the vendors, through lack of training or knowledge, were erroneously sending away customers.

The Licensing Division asked Sally Jagnandan, a DNR employee, to conduct a Green Hat thinking session. They wanted to develop other ways to reduce call volume without treating their vendors harshly. From the Green Hat session came several good ideas: sending vendors to a statewide training session, creating a CD-ROM training program, developing a vendor education manual, etc. The Division decided that the vendor manual would be the most practical solution.

They continued using the Six Thinking Hats to design the manual. The group worried that vendors wouldn't take the time to read the manual cover-to-cover, so they developed a simple, quick-reference guide. The training manual was a much more constructive approach to the problem than another round of corrective letters. Since the release of the manual, the DNR phone operators have reported a decline in the number of calls received each day.

The DNR's use of the Six Thinking Hats did not stop there. In September of the same year, the DNR decided to reinstate its Diversity Task Force, which consisted of one volunteer representative from each of the DNR's 17 bureaus. Because this group was starting up again after two years of inactivity, they needed to reestablish their purpose and goals. The taskforce was first and foremost dedicated to diversity in the workplace, but was now also interested in addressing quality issues, such as education and communication. Due to this additional focus, several members suggested the group change their name to "The Task Force for Workplace Quality and Diversity."

When this suggestion was made, no one imagined it would result in gridlock. Instead of a simple vote on the name change, members were solidly divided about whether to keep the original name. The September meeting was adjourned with no decision.

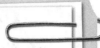

Fortunately, DNR employee Jerah Gallinger was on this task force and had also been trained in Six Thinking Hats. He decided to email a Six Thinking Hats worksheet to each task force member. The worksheet asked for Yellow and Black Hat thoughts regarding the name change. It also asked for Green Hat alternative ideas. Jerah created an electronic compilation of all the Black and Yellow Hat comments—keeping the names anonymous—and sent it to everyone. This allowed each person the opportunity to read the comments without the interference of tone of voice or passion, had the comments been spoken aloud. Jerah had developed a more controlled and less biased means of steering the process.

At the next meeting, everyone arrived ready to vote. By reading through the opinions prior to the meeting, the decision-making process was streamlined. The task force unanimously decided to keep their original name. Everyone was glad to get past the name issue and move on to making important decisions about quality and diversity in the workplace.

Summary:

ABN AMRO used Six Thinking Hats to help employees generate and present new ideas to top management.

Challenge:

• Encourage employees to produce more ideas

Method:

• Create the "Golden Idea" program incorporating Six Thinking Hats

Result:

• Employee ideas jump from 60 to 900 in one year

The Story:

ABN AMRO is a prominent international bank with 3,000 branches in 60 countries. In 2001, Mary Lou Leistikow, a Certified de Bono Instructor with QréaCom, was at a conference when an ABN AMRO manager approached her with a challenge. The Dutch branch of ABN AMRO employed more than 7,000 people, yet their employee suggestion box averaged merely 60 suggestions per year. This particular manager felt certain that the employees would offer more opinions and suggestions if creativity became a higher priority. They discussed the issue at some length, and the manager asked Mary Lou to make ABN AMRO more creative.

Mary Lou's first action was to get rid of the suggestion box. Then she went to the top managers and asked them for a commitment to creativity. She proposed a program called "The Golden Idea" to encourage innovation among employees. Mary Lou explained the benefit of taking the employees' ideas seriously, and she asked the managers to commit to implementing one new idea per quarter. They agreed.

To implement "The Golden Idea" Mary Lou held three half-day Green Hat sessions with 20 employees at a time. She wanted to teach a small group of employees about creativity, hoping that they would spread the word to the rest of the company. During the half-day sessions, the employees generated 300 completely new ideas that would improve business. This was a great start to the new program.

Each quarter, the management team asked specific questions about a particular topic, such as, "How can we use the Internet more with our customers?" or "How can we improve communication within the branch?" An internal web page was set up as a way for employees to quickly submit ideas. Within the first year, employees had more than 600 ideas listed, partly because the website was such a convenient repository.

Each quarter, a creative team sifted through all the ideas and selected the ten best. Then, they used the Six Thinking Hats to decide which five ideas to present to the senior managers. The managers then chose which idea to implement. Because the senior leadership team had committed to evaluate the ideas and implement the best one, employees finally felt as though they had an effective vehicle through which to voice their opinions.

There have been numerous topics and hundreds of ideas exchanged since "The Golden Idea" began. ABN AMRO continues to improve its customer care and internal strength with the assistance of its employees and their Green Hat suggestions.

"I just got lost in thought.
It was unfamiliar territory"

— Unknown

Summary:

Connex used Six Thinking Hats and Lateral Thinking to develop leadership competencies in employees identified as high-potential company leaders.

Challenges:

- Develop leadership skills in employees

- Reengineer business processes

Methods:

- Teach Six Thinking Hats and Lateral Thinking to increase leadership abilities

- Included Six Thinking Hats in a reengineering program

Results:

- Targeted employees developed the required leadership competencies

- Saw tremendous changes in customer sales, service and retention

The Story:

Connex holds 54% of Romania's mobile telecom-
munications market, and their network covers 80%
of the country and 95% of Romania's population. The
company was founded in 1997 and had anticipated
25,000 activations in its first year; instead it received
100,000. For three consecutive years, *The Economist*
recognized Connex as the "Best Company in Romania."
However, Connex realized that sustaining its position as
the market leader would require a great deal of creativity
and innovation.

In 1999, Connex identified a number of employees with
high potential to become company leaders and wanted
to develop their leadership skills. However, Romania
had adopted the free market only 10 years prior, so even
bright, well-educated employees had little experience
with the skills necessary to compete successfully in the
free market.

Connex Human Resources Director Valerie McGee
explained their challenge to Denyse Lynch, a certified de
Bono instructor. According to Valerie, the company needed
its leaders to be creative, risk-taking entrepreneurs,
capable of making sound decisions and empowering
others. Additionally, she hoped to get people thinking and
working together to face the new business challenges of
the post-communist era.

Connex choose two pilot groups of potential leaders to be
trained in Six Thinking Hats and Lateral Thinking. Denyse
recommended they first be trained in Six Thinking Hats to

develop their ability to think and work together, followed by Lateral Thinking to develop their creative abilities.

Each of the pilot groups participated in one week of Six Thinking Hats training followed by one week of Lateral Thinking training.

At the end of each session, Denyse asked participants to complete a detailed evaluation on the methods. She then summarized the evaluations and shared the feedback with senior management. This enabled them to gauge the success of training initiatives against their requirements for developing leadership competencies. The evaluations overwhelmingly indicated that the training was meeting the requirements. Additional de Bono training was requested, this time with cross-functional groups. Over the next two years, Denyse conducted many more training sessions as well as application workshops. Results showed that the company benefited greatly from the tools, so Denyse recommended that Connex train one of its employees to teach the tools to the rest of the organization. This would promote ownership and commitment to the tools, and it would also support Connex's business strategy of market leadership. Consequently, Simona Popovici, Director of Organizational Development and Employee Communication, became certified to teach Six Thinking Hats.

Simona wanted to apply the Six Thinking Hats to specific issues and then track the outcomes. With management endorsement, she instituted the Six Thinking Hats as a fundamental element of the new Business Process Reengineering initiative. Simona knew that the results would further engage the support of senior management and would motivate employees to use the tools.

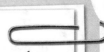

The new initiative entailed analysis of the changing market conditions and the rapid growth of the customer base. This led an executive team to identify 13 processes to be reengineered. Each member of the executive team took one process and led a cross functional team through an exploration of ways to redesign and improve the process in order to meet new business objectives. Some of the objectives included customer service, activation process, retention process and bad debt process.

The results of the process improvements were evident. The average speed of answer to customer service calls was reduced from 225 seconds to 40 seconds. The average amount of customer calls received per month went from 3 to 1.2. Activation time was reduced from 8 hours to 15 minutes. Voluntary customer churn rate was reduced by more than 50%. Bad debt was reduced from 4% to 2.18%.

In conjunction with this successful initiative, Simona sponsored "Innovation Day"—an event designed to publicly recognize employees who used the tools consistently and correctly. This positive recognition included a description of how the employees' use of Six Thinking Hats and Lateral Thinking had improved Connex, and Simona guessed that this would encourage more employees to get involved with the de Bono methods.

The awards ceremony was the highlight of the day, as numerous employees were acknowledged for using Six Thinking Hats and Lateral Thinking in their daily work setting. During Innovation Day, employees identified additional barriers to innovation. They generated Green Hat suggestions leading to an action plan to overcome those barriers.

The senior managers were pleased with the success of Innovation Day and the new level of creativity that had been sparked within the organization after using Six Thinking Hats in the reengineering project. They were so pleased, in fact, that they decided to certify four more Connex employees as de Bono trainers. Senior management's support led Connex to adopt and implement the tools quickly, which transformed the entire organization. The high-potential employees started transitioning into leadership positions better equipped and confident in their skills.

"Too often we enjoy the comfort of opinion without the discomfort of thought."

— John F. Kennedy

Summary:

Hewlett-Packard used Six Thinking Hats and Lateral Thinking to help organize a strategic planning meeting.

Challenge:

• To create a new plan in line with Hewlett-Packard's corporate goals

Method:

• Use Six Thinking Hats and Lateral Thinking to guide the strategic planning meeting for the Process and Quality Management Network Storage Solutions team

Result:

• Group dynamics improve and everyone agrees on a final strategy

The Story:

Hewlett-Packard is a leading global provider of technological solutions to consumers, businesses and institutions. On May 3, 2003, Hewlett-Packard merged with Compaq Computer Corporation. This was the largest technology merger in history. Following the merger, Hewlett-Packard's 142,000 employees conducted business in 40 currencies across 160 countries.

The company wanted to complete the merger without losing focus on customers. Various teams within the company were asked to create strategic plans in line with Hewlett-Packard's corporate goals. In these strategic planning meetings, each team member would present his or her business plan. However, poor group dynamics, partly due to the merger, prevented the groups from moving forward. Power struggles were interfering with team cohesion.

The team for Process and Quality Management Network Storage Solutions was having an especially difficult time working together to draft a plan. Team member Jon Albregts was given the task of organizing the strategic planning meeting. Jon had previously attended a de Bono workshop led by Master Trainer Mike Sproul, so he called Mike for advice. Together Jon and Mike mapped out a solid plan for the meeting. The team would first be sent pre-meeting work via email. This email would outline the overall goals of the group and ask the team members to present only White Hat information on their business plan.

The pre-meeting work was useful, and everyone arrived at the meeting ready to present the White Hat information.

Following the presentations, the group used the Yellow and Black Hats to analyze each initiative. Next, they engaged in a Lateral Thinking session to find alternative solutions and ideas. Then they used the Red Hat to express gut feelings about the initiative. Finally, the Blue Hat helped them identify the next steps for implementing the plan.

Six Thinking Hats provided the insight the team needed to move initiatives forward. Team members were amazed that the usual, tired arguments and debates didn't pop up in this particular meeting. Never before had the team accomplished so much so quickly to everyone's satisfaction

Six Thinking Hats and Lateral Thinking have been used as part of the Hewlett-Packard quality initiative for several years now, and the success of the de Bono tools has spread to other divisions of the Hewlett-Packard/Compaq conglomerate.

"The significant problems we face cannot be solved at the same level of thinking we were at when we created them"

— Albert Einstein

Summary:

Motorola used Six Thinking Hats and Lateral Thinking to develop a high-tech, hand-held communications device.

Challenges:

- Create an ultra high-tech device with the price tag of less than $800

Methods:

- Use Concept Generation, Concept Extraction, Reverse Provocation, Random Object and Six Thinking Hats to develop the ideal product

Results:

- Motorola develops and markets the Accompli 009 Personal Communicator

The Story:

Motorola is a global leader in communications technologies. Motorola already manufactured a product for people who make time management a priority. Another product targeted people whose top priority is keeping in touch with friends and relatives. A third product, often purchased by the rich and famous, was aimed at "status seekers."

But in 2002, Motorola wanted to create a "product for the future."

The company planned a three-day event for its product managers with the focus of developing a new high-tech, hand-held device for people who want cutting edge technology, but don't want to spend more than $800. To ensure that the event went as smoothly as possible, Motorola decided to enlist the help of Master Trainer Jay Wenberg.

On the first day, consumer profiles, based on exhaustive research, were constructed for each existing product. Product presentation and framing with regional perspective was offered to the group. The goal of the first day was for product managers to gain detailed understanding of each product's target market. They discussed every aspect of the consumers' traits, including age, income, educational background, cultural beliefs and daily habits. This gave the managers a detailed picture of Motorola's customers.

The second day began with a "technology soak," which defined the capabilities and limitations of existing technology. Then Jay gave an overview of the Six Thinking Hats and Lateral Thinking. He led the group through a Green Hat ssession in order to generate ideas for the "product for the future."

During the Green Hat session, the group used the Lateral Thinking technique of Reverse Provocation to challenge the physical limitations of technology. Jay handed out trinkets from a dime store to assist in a Random Objects exercise. After all Green Hat ideas had been offered, each one was evaluated using Yellow and Black Hat thinking. Finally, the group used Red Hat thinking to prioritize the best ideas.

The final result of the Green Hat session was a technologically advanced product called the Accompli. The device functioned as a mobile business tool or "virtual office" complete with a full keyboard. Its wireless network connection provided fast Internet access across the globe. In addition, consumers could install additional business applications on the Accompli and even play an assortment of games.

The group then took the White Hat information gathered from the consumer profiles to practice a "day in the life" of an Accompli owner. They discussed how consumers might use the new device from the time they woke up to the time they went to bed. The team noted all the additional features the Accompli might need to make the user's life easier. For instance, could it have an alarm? Could it play MP3 music files? What should the greeting sound like? The group dissected the consumer's day hour by hour to ensure that the Accompli was the idea product for the target market.

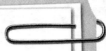

At the end of the event, the product managers were excited about the outcome of their hard work, and even people who didn't attend the event heard about its success. Shortly thereafter, Motorola introduced the Accompli in North America, Europe and Asia.

Summary:

3M used Six Thinking Hats to create products for new markets.

Challenges:

- Design a filtration device for a new market

- Improve duct tape

Methods:

- Use Red Hat to find top priorities

- Use Six Thinking Hats to establish new duct tape product

Results:

- Patent is filed for filtration device

- Duct tape for women is available in the market

The Story:

3M is an 18 billion dollar company that offers an incredibly wide range of products. The firm is an industry leader in such diverse fields as health care, office products and transportation. 3M manufactures familiar products, like Post-it® Notes and Scotch® tape, and the firm is one of the 30 blue-chip companies that constitute the Dow Jones Industrial Average.

3M's filtration unit makes filters for cars, buses and airplanes. When the filtration unit discovered a new market opportunity, they wanted to quickly design a new product. They put together a team of employees from both marketing and product development, and the team hoped to choose the final concept at the end of a one-day meeting. The team generated ten good ideas but did not know how to proceed from there.

Kim Johnson, from 3M's Corporate Research and Development, had previously attended a Six Thinking Hats course. Recalling the benefits of the Hats, Kim decided to conduct a Six Thinking Hats session with the team. Each individual gave input on the ten ideas, narrowing the priorities to the most popular ideas. The team chose its favorite idea, and since that time, 3M has filed for a patent for the new filter.

Later, Kim was asked to assist the Construction and Home Improvement Department, which, among other products, is responsible for duct tape.

Through market research the department learned that people used duct tape in a host of unusual ways, from constructing a wallet made of duct tape to holding a car door in place. The department recognized that there was a cult of duct tape enthusiasts around the world, and it wanted to broaden its market with an updated or innovative version of duct tape. To work on this challenge, the department asked Kim to lead three half-day Six Thinking Hats sessions with concept ideation experts.

The first session focused on the Green Hat, and participants gave ideas for a new version of duct tape. In the second session, Kim divided the team into smaller groups and asked them to discuss each of the ideas using the Yellow and Black Hats. In the final session, the group used Red Hat to determine which ideas were the favorites. After the third session, the department decided on the new product: duct tape for women. Rather than the industrial gray color of original duct tape, this version would be a colorful variation. This product is now on the market, thanks in part to the Six Thinking Hats.

"There is no doubt
that creativity is the
most important human
resource of all.
Without creativity, there
would be no progress, and
we would be forever
repeating the
same patterns"

— Edward de Bono

Summary:

ABB used the Six Thinking Hats to create a shortcut in the decision-making process, design a communications tool and enter a closed market.

Challenges:

- Simplify decision-making process
- Improve internal communications
- Meet market needs and secure business

Methods:

- Implement Six Thinking Hats in meetings where key decisions are discussed
- Use Six Thinking Hats template for internal communications
- Use Six Thinking Hats in all company presentations regarding needs and challenges

Results:

- Decision making time is cut by 60%
- Internal communications are standardized through use of a common language
- Profit in the Syrian market goes from zero to $60 million in two years

The Story:

The ABB Group is a world leader in power and automation technologies, which enable utility and industry customers to improve performance while reducing environmental impact. ABB employs 113,000 people and operates in more than 100 countries.

At a de Bono workshop in 1996, Certified de Bono Instructor Dina Faidi met the ABB regional manager in charge of Jordan, Syria, Lebanon and Palestine. This manager was particularly interested in improving his region's performance in internal meetings, communications and market assessment. He invited Dina to train the ABB managers in these four countries in the use of the Six Thinking Hats.

Dina conducted a series of Six Thinking Hats workshops with the ABB managers. After the training, they started using the tool in their daily meetings. According to the regional manager, this cut decision-making time by an astounding 60%.

The regional manager also developed a communications tool based on the Six Thinking Hats. It was a one-page template with the hat colors, and managers in all four countries were expected to use it for all reports, proposals or suggestions. This template was also used for all management presentations. In short, all internal communications were filtered through the Six Thinking Hats, making it simpler for departments to convey ideas.

In keeping with this practice, the regional manager used the Six Thinking Hats to overcome a significant challenge in Syria. The Syrian market was large and held lots of potential, but ABB faced fierce competition there. The regional manager convened a meeting and asked participants to use the Green Hat to think of a completely new and different approach to the Syria challenge. The team realized that ABB had overlooked several other potential resources other than the one who had unsuccessfully pursued Syrian business opportunities for the previous eight years. A new suggestion was presented to the management using the Six Thinking Hats. It received executive approval, and ABB entered the Syrian market. ABB had made zero profit in Syria in the previous eight years, but only two years after the aforementioned meeting, the company had already earned a $60 million profit.

"A great many people think they are thinking when they are merely rearranging their prejudices"

— William James

Summary:

MDS Sciex used Six Thinking Hats to streamline the design and production process for their new product, QSTAR™.

Challenge:

- Move a new product quickly through the design process and put it on the market as soon as possible

Method:

- Use Six Thinking Hats to create an objective atmosphere in design review meetings and increase team collaboration

Result:

- Product enters the market in one year, instead of the usual 2 ½ to 4 years, and production costs are reduced by $35,000 per unit

The Story:

MDS Sciex is a world leader in the research, design and manufacture of mass spectrometers, which are scientific instruments used to detect and analyze minute quantities of chemical compounds. Mass spectrometers are frequently used for environmental and medical purposes, such as analyzing the pollution level of a river or testing a blood sample for illegal substances.

Scientific instruments evolve rapidly, so it is important for MDS Sciex to quickly transform ideas into products. However, design review meetings were often plagued by a breakdown of collaboration and teamwork. Because the scientists and engineers had put so much time and energy into new design concepts, they took it personally when their colleagues critiqued those concepts during the review meetings. This strained team relations, and projects plodded along or sometimes stopped altogether.

In 1998, MDS Sciex was in the process of developing a mass spectrometer called QSTAR. This was an extremely accurate, cutting-edge product aimed at the pharmaceutical market, but the team was unsure how to get the product to market quickly enough to capture the market segment. To further complicate the situation, one of MDS Sciex's competitors had already released a similar product, so they needed to act fast.

In 1998, MDS Sciex employees received training on the Six Thinking Hats from MICA, a Toronto-based consulting company. Certified de Bono Trainer Patti Thompson led the session, and the group began to use the Six Thinking Hats in QSTAR daily design meetings. Much to the amazement of the project manager, the Six Thinking Hats cut the meeting time in half. Moreover, the design review process became more transparent and objective. The bickering and personal attacks ceased. The team evaluated concepts in a nonadversarial manner, giving both constructive criticism under Black Hat and positive encouragement under Yellow Hat. Team members felt free to share and build on others' ideas, and creative energy began to flow.

After the team members finally started to collaborate, the product development cycle went much faster than usual. In addition, the team found ways to add functionality while simplifying the manufacturing, which cut material costs by $35,000 per unit. By the time the QSTAR entered production, most of the problems involving reliability had already been addressed, and the scientists were stunned to have so little involvement in the manufacturing stage. The first QSTAR was produced just one year after the design process began. In the past, similar product launches had taken 2 ½ to 4 years, and the scientists were deeply involved until the second year of production.

Not only was product development streamlined, but the Human Resources Director also reported that Six Thinking Hats brought an enormous cultural change to the company. Using the Six Thinking Hats, the employees of MDS Sciex eliminated criticism and confrontation from their environment, and they learned to build on each other's ideas to create a more solid and successful workplace.

"What luck for rulers that men do not think."

-Adolph Hitler

Summary:

The Manganese Metal Company used Six Thinking Hats to regain their share in the market and handle a waste management issue.

Challenges:

- Respond to a drop in market share

- Prove to the government that all waste management options have been researched

Methods:

- Use Six Thinking Hats to develop a comprehensive plan to help the company stay competitive with Chinese firms

- Have a meeting structured with Six Thinking Hats in which waste management options can be shared and discussed

Results:

- Company remains selenium-free while maintaining market share

- Managers draft an 18-page report on waste management options in only one day

The Story:

The Manganese Metal company's South African division is the world's largest producer of electrolytic manganese, a component of tin. Electrolytic manganese is a specialized product, and it is mined only in South Africa and China.

Production of electrolytic manganese is both cheaper and faster if selenium is added to the process. Although selenium itself is harmless, certain selenium compounds are extremely toxic. To protect its employees, MMC had never used selenium in electrolytic manganese production, but MMC's Chinese competitors did not face this regulation. As a result, Chinese firms enjoyed a cost advantage of $150 per ton over South African firms, including MMC. This led to a market decline for MMC and the other South African producers.

MMC's leaders asked Master Trainer Nicola Tyler to help with this problem. She began by leading a Blue Hat session in which managers decided that they could remain competitive by reducing China's cost advantage. The managers identified two ways to accomplish this: through selenium regulation in China and through consumer knowledge about the dangers of selenium-based production.

Next, Nicola led a White Hat session. Experts presented technical information about selenium to the group. Then the participants broke into small groups for Green Hat thinking. Those sessions yielded 265 ideas, which the group evaluated and prioritized using the Black and Yellow Hats. By the end of the session, the group had produced a strategy to influence Chinese regulatory policy and to educate consumers about the dangers of selenium. They accomplished this through a presentation at a global conference and by publishing follow-up reports. Currently, MMC is helping the Chinese government to revise its selenium regulations. MMC also maintains an online resource center to raise consumer awareness.

MMC asked Nicola to assist with a waste management issue. Waste management in South Africa had never been properly regulated, and frequently, industrial waste was dumped improperly and contaminated the water supply. The South African government had recently introduced much stricter environmental legislation, mandating that firms dispose of their waste material in the most optimal way. Under the new regulations, MMC needed to prove that its waste management decisions were based on thorough research and considered a broad range of disposal options.

MMC arranged a meeting between its managers, its technical team, its lawyers, waste management consultants, and environmental activists. Nicola facilitated the meeting using the Six Thinking Hats. She began with the Blue Hat in order to define the meeting's focus: to devise a waste management plan that everyone could support. Each party gave a White Hat presentation on waste management from its perspective: legal, environmental, technical, etc. Following these presentations, Nicola asked the group for Green Hat ideas. One suggestion, for example, was that MMC could incinerate waste before disposing of it.

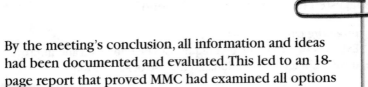

By the meeting's conclusion, all information and ideas had been documented and evaluated. This led to an 18-page report that proved MMC had examined all options and met government requirements. Instead of months of research, MMC got input from all parties in just a single day. Everyone involved was satisfied with the final waste management decision.

Appendix A

Suggested reading by Edward de Bono:

Breaking Out Of The Box
Explains that thinking techniques can be enhanced and improved through practice, attention and the use of simple tools.

I Am Right, You Are Wrong
Challenges the monopoly that logic has always held on Western though by explaining alternative methods to arguments, absolutes and point scoring.

Lateral Thinking
Teaches the expansion of creative powers by "thinking sideways"—a proven, effective method for helping the human mind function as a creative tool.

The Mechanism of the Mind
Dr. Edward de Bono's first book that details his research of the brain's self-organizing systems, which later led to the development of his creative thinking methods.

Serious Creativity
Describes the process and art of creative thinking, and summarizes 25 years of practical experience in the deliberate use of creativity.

Six Thinking Hats
Teaches how to maximize the mind's effectiveness and improve group collaborative efforts by separating thinking into six distinct modes.

Additional resource:

Total Creativity
David Tanner, founder of the DuPont Center for Creativity and Innovation, lays out an experiential-based road map for using the de Bono Methods to change corporate culture.

If you are interested in training courses by Edward de Bono, visit www.aptt.com.

General Index

A

ABB - 78,79
ABN AMRO - 56,57
Ad sales - 24, 25, 26
Advertising - 24, 25, 26, 33
A.G.O. - 7
Airplane manufacturing - 9
Alternatives - 5
A.P.C. - 7
Arabian Gulf - 41

B

Banking - 57
Black Hat - 3,12,14,15,18,33,37,55,68,72,76,84,96
Blouch, Susan - 21,22
Blue Hat - 3,15,18,67,87,88,96
Boeing - 8,9

C

C & S - 7,37
CAF - 7,37,41
Canada - 9,25,45
Casino - 12,13,14,15
Challenge - 5
Computer Sciences Corporation - 21
Connex - 60,61,62,63,64
Counseling - 28,29,30
Courtroom - 50

D

DATT - 1,6,7,36,37,38,40,41,42
Department of Natural Resources - 52,53,54
Diversity - 52,54,55
DOCA - 7
Duct Tape - 74,75,76

Results Index

Stories in which the de Bono tools were used to:

About the Author

Barbara Stennes, CSP (Certified Speaking Professional) is the president and owner of Resources Unlimited, a consulting firm based in Des Moines, Iowa. She has consulted with over 70,000 people in hundreds of organizations across North America, South America and Europe. For the last 20 years, Barbara has owned and operated Resources Unlimited plus two other businesses, with responsibilities in business development, marketing, human resources and operations.

Dr. Edward de Bono personally trained and certified Barbara to facilitate seminars on creativity, innovation and thinking skills. In 2002, Barbara was one of three certified trainers to receive a special award entitled "Lifetime Certified Master Trainer" for her 10 years of outstanding leadership in Edward de Bono's Global Network.

Barbara earned the Certified Speaking Professional title from the National Speakers Association and has received numerous sales and leadership awards from other organizations. She also served as president of the Iowa chapter of the American Society for Training and Development and has held board positions for various other organizations.

The Resources Unlimited client list includes organizations such as Bristol Myers Squibb, Gap, General Electric, Mayo Clinic, Meredith Publishing, Novartis, Pillsbury, Pfizer, Pioneer Hi-Bred International, Principal Financial Group, Robert Bosch, the U.S. Army, the U.S. Department of Energy, Wells Fargo and many others worldwide.

Barbara is working on a sequel to this book. If you would like to be interviewed, she would enjoy hearing from you. You may contact her at:

Barbara.Stennes@ResourcesUnlimited.com